THE ULTIMATE 10

Natural Disasters

VOLCANOES

By Jayne Keedle

Gareth Stevens
Publishing

Please visit our web site at www.garethstevens.com.
For a free catalog describing Gareth Stevens Publishing's list of high-quality books,
call 1-800-542-2595 (USA) or 1-800-387-3178 (Canada).
Gareth Stevens Publishing's fax: 1-877-542-2596

Library of Congress Cataloging-in-Publication Data
Keedle, Jayne.
    Volcanoes / by Jayne Keedle.
        p. cm. — (Ultimate 10 : natural disasters)
    Includes bibliographical references and index.
    ISBN-13: 978-0-8368-9155-3 (lib. bdg. : alk. paper)
    ISBN-10: 0-8368-9155-4 (lib. bdg. : alk. paper)
    1. Volcanoes—Juvenile literature. I. Title.
    QE521.3.K44   2009
    551.21—dc22   2008018952

This edition first published in 2009 by
Gareth Stevens Publishing
A Weekly Reader® Company
1 Reader's Digest Rd.
Pleasantville, NY 10570-7000 USA

Copyright © 2009 by Gareth Stevens, Inc.

Senior Managing Editor: Lisa M. Herrington
Senior Editor: Brian Fitzgerald
Creative Director: Lisa Donovan
Senior Designer: Keith Plechaty
Photo Researcher: Charlene Pinckney
Special thanks to Joann Jovinelly

Numbers of deaths and injuries from
natural disasters vary from source to
source, particularly for disasters that struck
long ago. The figures included in this book
are based on the best information available
from the most reliable sources.

Picture credits:
Key: t = top, c = center, b = bottom.
Cover, title page: Shutterstock; pp. 4–5: Shutterstock; p. 7: (t) AP, (b) Gianni Dagli Orti/Art Archive; p. 8: (t) Jay Directo/
AFP/Getty Images, (c) NASA/Photo Researchers, (b) © Corbis; p. 9: (t) Peter W. Lipman/U.S. Geological Survey, (c)
Cheryl Nuss/National Geographic/Getty Images, (b) Shutterstock, (volcano illustration) Bill Melvin; p 11: (t) Hulton
Archive/Getty Images, (b) AP; p. 12: (b) NASA; p. 13: (t) Ed Wray/AP, (b) Shutterstock; p. 15: (t, b) Courtesy of
University of Rhode Island; p. 17: (t, c) Courtesy University of Rhode Island, (b) © Bettmann/Corbis; p. 19: (t) Mike
Doukas/U.S. Geological Survey, (b) Robert Madden/National Geographic/Getty Images; p. 20: (t) D. Dzurisin/U.S.
Geological Survey, (c, b) Harry Glicken/U.S. Geological Survey; p. 21: (t) Steve Schilling-Dan Dzurisin/U.S. Geological
Survey, (b) Harry Glicken/U.S. Geological Survey; p. 23: (t) © Alfio Scigliano/Sygma/Corbis, (b) Hulton Archive/
Getty Images; p. 24: (t) NASA, (b) Pier Paolo/AP; p. 25: (t) Fabrizio/AP, (b) © Alfio Scigliano/Sygma/Corbis;
p. 27: (t) U.S. Geological Survey, (b) R.T. Holcomb/Corbis; p. 28: (t) G. Brad Lewis/Getty Images, (b) Shutterstock;
p. 29: (t) R. B. Moore/U.S. Geological Survey, (c) NASA, (b) Shutterstock; p. 31: (t) Douglas Peebles/Digital Railroad,
(b) J.D. Griggs /Corbis; p. 32: (t) © Roger Ressmeyer/Corbis, (b) © Linda Reinink-Smith/Alamy; p. 33: (t) SeaPics,
(b) Herb Kawainui Kane; p. 35: (t) NPS, (b) Tom Murphy/National Geographic/Getty Images; p. 36: (b) Joe Scherschel/
National Geographic/Getty Images; p. 37: (t) Shutterstock; p. 39: (t) © Alberto Garcia/Corbis, (b) © Les Stone/Sygma/
Corbis; p. 40: (t) © Roger Ressmeyer/Corbis, (b) John Ewert/U.S. Geological Survey; p. 41: (t) Itsuo Inouye/AP, (c)
Bullit Marquez/AP, (b) Joanna B. Pinneo/Aurora/Getty Images; p. 43: (t) U.S. Geological Survey; p. 44: © Emmanuel
Lattes/Alamy, (inset) JTB Photo/Alamy; p. 45: (t) Wesley Boxce/Getty Images, (b) © Corbis; p. 46: (t) Henry Guttmann/
Getty Images, (c) AP, (b) NASA/JPL.

All maps by Keith Plechaty

Printed in the United States of America

1 2 3 4 5 6 7 8 9 10 09 08

Table of Contents

Words in the glossary appear in **bold** type
the first time they are used in the text.

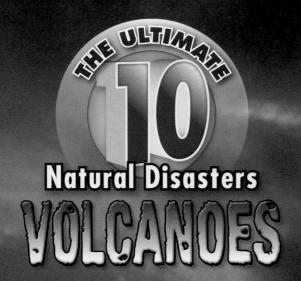

THE ULTIMATE 10

Natural Disasters

VOLCANOES

Welcome to The Ultimate 10! This exciting series explores Earth's most powerful and unforgettable natural disasters.

In this book, you'll get an inside look at volcanoes: how they form, the damage they cause when they blow their tops, and what scientists are doing to predict future eruptions.

No force of nature is as powerful as a volcano. A volcano is an opening in Earth's **crust** that blasts out molten (melted) rock, ash, and gas. Volcanoes erupt when heat and pressure build up deep inside Earth.

Volcanic eruptions have shaped Earth, changed the climate, and wiped out whole cities. Volcanoes also create, however. Molten rock cools to form new land. Volcanic ash becomes rich soil.

Today, there are about 1,500 active volcanoes on Earth. But even a sleeping giant can rumble back to life at any time—with devastating effects.

Rocking the World

Here's a look at 10 volcanoes that have rocked the world.

 Mount Vesuvius, Italy

 Krakatau, Indonesia

 Mount Tambora, Indonesia

 Mount St. Helens, Washington

 Mount Etna, Italy

 Mauna Loa, Hawaii

 Kilauea, Hawaii

 Yellowstone Caldera, Idaho, Montana, Wyoming

 Mount Pinatubo, Philippines

 Parícutin, Mexico

#1

Mount Vesuvius
Most Famous Volcano on Earth

One of the deadliest volcanoes on Earth can be found in southern Italy. Mount Vesuvius last erupted in 1944, but its most famous eruption happened nearly 2,000 years ago. In A.D. 79, Vesuvius exploded with huge force. Two ancient Roman cities were sealed in time. Today, Vesuvius threatens the lives of more than 3 million people. Many of them live in nearby Naples.

FAST FACTS

Mount Vesuvius

Location: Naples, Italy

Type: Composite volcano

Height: 4,202 feet (1,281 m)

Last Eruption: 1944

ASIA

Atlantic Ocean

Italy

Vesuvius

AFRICA

Ash shot out from Mount Vesuvius during the 1944 eruption. Scientists think Vesuvius has erupted as many as 40 times since A.D. 79.

Violent Vesuvius

During the A.D. 79 eruption, dark clouds of ash and gases rose about 20 miles (32 kilometers) into the sky. Hot volcanic rock rained down on the city of Pompeii. Death came in an instant. Hot ash burned people where they stood. The explosion buried the city under layers of hot ash and volcanic rock up to 23 feet (7 meters) deep.

Buried Alive

All of Pompeii was sealed with ash. Over time, the ash cooled and hardened. The bodies of people and animals rotted away, leaving hollow shells. Scientists filled the hollow shells with plaster. The plaster casts show the positions in which people and animals died.

The A.D. 79 eruption froze this man in this position.

Ready to Rumble

Volcanoes come in different shapes and sizes. Their shape depends on how they are formed and the way molten rock erupts. Molten rock is called **magma** until it reaches the surface. Then it's called **lava**. There are three main types of volcanoes: composite, shield, and cinder cone.

Vesuvius is a composite volcano. This type of volcano is cone-shaped. Composite volcanoes often have steep sloping sides and rise thousands of feet high.

Composite volcanoes are built from layers of lava and ash.

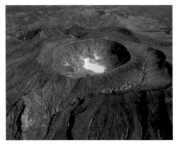

Shield volcanoes form when repeated eruptions of lava spread over a wide area.

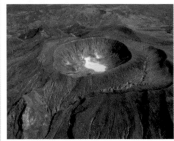

Cinder cone volcanoes form when ash and rock, not lava, fall around the vent.

LAVA
magma that flows onto Earth's surface, cools, and hardens into rock

CRATER
the opening at the top of a volcano

layers of lava and ash

SIDE VENTS
openings in a volcano where magma, ash, and steam can escape

CRUST
Earth's hard outer layer

MAGMA CHAMBER
an underground area of thick, molten rock

CENTRAL VENT
the main channel in the neck of a volcano through which magma rises

Gone With the Flow

The city of Herculaneum suffered a different fate in A.D. 79. The huge eruption cloud that showered Pompeii collapsed the next day. Scalding-hot rocks, ash, and mud barreled down the mountain like an avalanche. The fast-moving **pyroclastic flow** buried Herculaneum under a thick layer of ash and mud.

A pyroclastic flow can be hotter than 900° Fahrenheit (482° Celsius).

Rediscovering the Past

The two ancient cities remained buried under rock and ash for centuries. The lost cities were rediscovered in the 1700s. **Archaeologists** continue to dig up the sites to this day. The ash that destroyed the cities also preserved them. Their buildings and **artifacts** offer clues about the lives of ancient Romans.

Archaeologists found the skeletons of about 250 people in boathouses at Herculaneum. They were waiting for rescue boats when they died.

Did You Know?

The volcano's deadly past hasn't stopped people from living on its slopes. The Italian government has paid people living near Vesuvius to move to safer places. Scientists are working on emergency plans for when the volcano erupts again.

9

#2 Krakatau
A Blast Heard Around the World

For two centuries, Krakatau in Indonesia had been quiet. That changed on August 26, 1883. At 12:53 P.M., an ear-splitting eruption shot a cloud of ash and rock miles into the sky. The following morning, four massive eruptions blew the volcanic island apart. People more than 2,800 miles (4,506 km) away heard the final explosion. By the time the rumbling ended, just one-third of Krakatau remained above sea level. More than 36,000 people were dead.

FAST FACTS

Krakatau

Location: Krakatau, Indonesia

Type: Three composite volcanoes

Height: 2,668 feet (813 m)

Last Eruption: 2008

ASIA

Pacific Ocean

Indonesia

Krakatau

Indian Ocean

AUSTRALIA

Killer Waves

No one lived on Krakatau, yet its eruption was deadly. Most of the volcano sank into the sea. This created **tsunamis**, giant waves that measured up to 100 feet (30 m) high. The killer waves raced toward Indonesia's populated islands of Java and Sumatra. Tsunamis wiped out about 165 villages.

This print shows hot ash shooting from Krakatau during the 1883 eruption.

The Scream

Krakatau's eruption created a gigantic volcanic cloud. The volcanic gases and ash affected weather worldwide. The famous painting *The Scream*, by Norwegian artist Edvard Munch, shows a blood-red sky. That vivid sunset may have been created by Krakatau—on the other side of the world.

Eyewitness

" Thousands of corpses of human beings and also carcasses of animals still await burial. They lie in knots and entangled masses impossible to unravel. **"**

— a visitor to a devastated village in Indonesia, two weeks after the eruption

How Volcanoes Form

Earth's crust, or hard outer layer, floats above a layer of magma. The crust is divided into huge sections called **tectonic plates**. Volcanoes often form where tectonic plates meet. Magma pushes up against the rock and escapes through cracks between the plates, forming volcanoes. Krakatau lies in the area where the Australian Plate sinks beneath the Eurasian Plate.

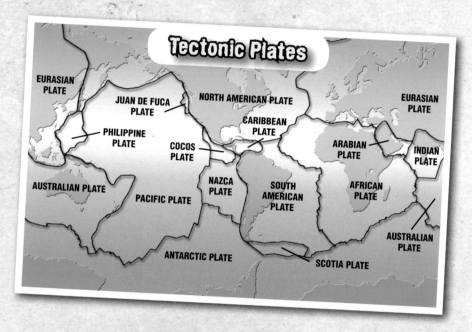

Tectonic Plates

EURASIAN PLATE

JUAN DE FUCA PLATE

NORTH AMERICAN PLATE

EURASIAN PLATE

PHILIPPINE PLATE

CARIBBEAN PLATE

COCOS PLATE

ARABIAN PLATE

INDIAN PLATE

AUSTRALIAN PLATE

NAZCA PLATE

SOUTH AMERICAN PLATE

AFRICAN PLATE

PACIFIC PLATE

AUSTRALIAN PLATE

ANTARCTIC PLATE

SCOTIA PLATE

Anak Krakatau

island before 1883 eruption

Krakatau

Krakatau Collapses

Krakatau was made up of three connected volcanoes. After the 1883 eruption, only half of one of them remained above sea level. The other two volcanoes collapsed. They formed a **caldera**, a bowl-shaped crater that filled with water.

Volcanic Child

In 1927, a small volcano appeared in the center of the Krakatau caldera. It was created by underwater eruptions. Lava and ash had hardened and formed a cone. This small but active volcano is called Anak Krakatau, or "child of Krakatau." Its many eruptions add new layers of volcanic ash and rock. Today, it is about 1,000 feet (305 m) tall and still growing.

Lava and ash continue to flow from Anak Krakatau. As the molten material hardens, the island gets bigger.

Did You Know?

Hot volcanic matter that shot from Krakatau cooled and hardened. It formed floating islands of pumice. This volcanic rock is full of tiny air bubbles, making it light enough to float. Some of these rafts of rock floated clear across the Indian Ocean. Others stayed afloat for two years.

#3 Mount Tambora
Deadliest Eruption in History

The 140,000 people who lived on the small island of Sumbawa never knew they were in danger. Mount Tambora had barely rumbled for 5,000 years. On April 5, 1815, the volcano awoke with a thunderous explosion. The result was the largest and deadliest eruption in recorded history. Tambora's vast ash cloud clogged the air. The eruption changed the world's climate for a year.

FAST FACTS

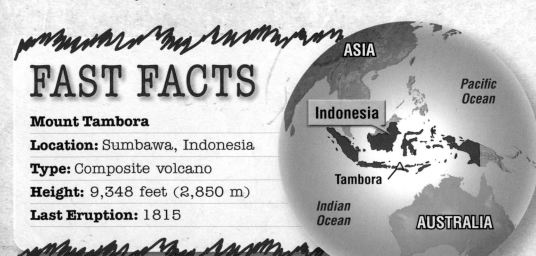

Mount Tambora

Location: Sumbawa, Indonesia

Type: Composite volcano

Height: 9,348 feet (2,850 m)

Last Eruption: 1815

ASIA

Pacific Ocean

Indonesia

Tambora

Indian Ocean

AUSTRALIA

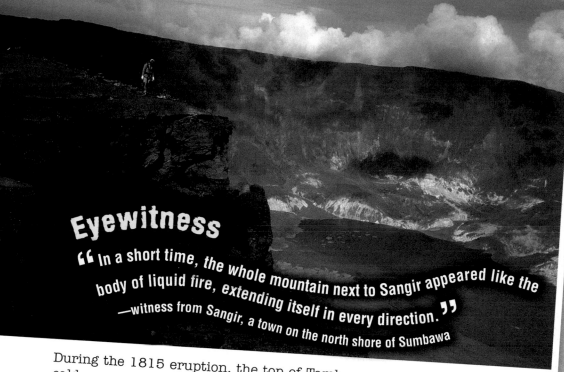

During the 1815 eruption, the top of Tambora collapsed. It left a caldera nearly 5 miles (8 km) wide and 4,100 feet (1,250 m) deep.

What's That Sound?

Some 200 miles (322 km) away, sailors aboard the warship *Benares* heard what sounded like cannon fire. What they heard was Tambora erupting. The volcano spewed 150 times more lava than the 1980 eruption of Mount St. Helens (see page 18).

Darkness and Death

The huge cloud of volcanic ash plunged the area into darkness. Lava flows buried villages. All plant life on the island was destroyed. In all, about 92,000 people died from the eruption and the famine that followed.

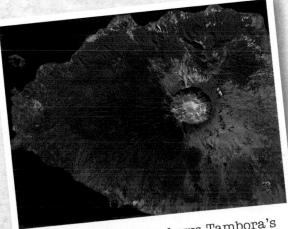

This satellite photo shows Tambora's giant caldera.

The Ring of Fire

Tambora is one of about 130 active volcanoes in Indonesia. That's more than any other country in the world. Indonesia is one of several countries that sit along the Ring of Fire. This region encircles the Pacific Ocean. It follows the borders of Earth's major tectonic plates. Most of the world's active volcanoes are in the Ring of Fire.

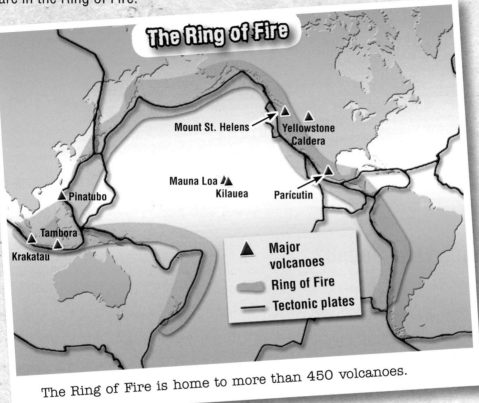

The Ring of Fire

Mount St. Helens

Yellowstone Caldera

Mauna Loa
Kilauea

Parícutin

Pinatubo

Tambora

Krakatau

▲ Major volcanoes

Ring of Fire

— Tectonic plates

The Ring of Fire is home to more than 450 volcanoes.

Top Five Deadliest Eruptions in History

Volcano	Year	Deaths
1. Tambora, Indonesia	1815	92,000
2. Krakatau, Indonesia	1883	36,417
3. Mont Pelée, Martinique	1902	29,025
4. Nevado del Ruiz, Colombia	1985	23,000
5. Unzen, Japan	1792	14,300

Source: volcano.und.edu

Pompeii of the East?
Tambora rained down molten rock and ash. The eruption froze its victims in place. In 2004, scientists discovered a house on Sumbawa buried under 10 feet (3 m) of ash. They found two bodies, pottery, and jewelry. The site offered clues into a lost Indonesian culture.

The Year Without a Summer

Tambora spat millions of tons of dust and gas into the sky. The gases blocked sunlight. The decrease in sunlight caused global temperatures to drop for more than a year. More than 9,000 miles (14,484 km) away from Tambora, several inches of snow fell in New England in June. Snow and frost killed most crops in the region. People in Europe and North America described 1816 as "the year without a summer."

Did You Know?

The gloomy weather in the summer of 1816 caused many people in Europe to stay indoors. During that dreary time, Mary Shelley was inspired to write the classic horror novel *Frankenstein*.

#4

Mount St. Helens
Deadliest U.S. Eruption of the 20th Century

On May 18, 1980, Mount St. Helens blasted apart. The eruption was the deadliest in the United States in the past century. Some 57 people and thousands of animals died in an avalanche of hot rocks and ash. Scientists had been monitoring the mountain for months before it erupted. They warned people of the danger. Even so, no one expected the mountain to collapse.

FAST FACTS

Mount St. Helens

Location: Washington state

Type: Composite volcano

Height: 8,364 feet (2,549 m)

Last Eruption: 2004

Washington

Mount St. Helens

NORTH AMERICA

Atlantic Ocean

Pacific Ocean

Blown Away

After more than a century of silence, the snowcapped Mount St. Helens began to rumble in March 1980. At 8:32 A.M. on May 18, it let out a huge bang. Within seconds, the north side of the volcano was blown apart.

Super-hot pyroclastic flows raced down the mountainside. The rivers of rock and ash wiped out trees and wildlife within 212 square miles (549 sq km) of the blast. It was the largest landslide in recorded history.

Huge Ash Cloud

After Mount St. Helens collapsed, a huge cloud of ash surged from within the volcano. In less than a half hour, the ash cloud was 10 miles (16 km) high.

Eyewitness

❝ You expect volcanoes to erupt, but you don't expect mountains to fall apart. ❞
— Dorothy Stoffel, a scientist who was flying over Mount St. Helens when it erupted

Ash from Mount St. Helens fell on Yakima, Washington, more than 90 miles (145 km) away.

Deadly Mix

As Mount St. Helens burst open, volcanic rock and ash melted the snow and ice on its slopes. This created deadly mudflows that wiped out homes, roads, and bridges.

Miles from Mount St. Helens, this car was buried by the volcano's mudflow.

BEFORE

Changing Shape
Before the eruption, the peak of Mount St. Helens rose 9,677 feet (2,950 m). The mountain's sides were thick with evergreen forests. The eruption blew off the top 1,313 feet (400 m). It wiped out forests and polluted lakes with ash and mud. The eruption lasted for more than nine hours and blew away a large chunk of the mountain.

AFTER

Crater left by eruption

Safety Zone

In 1980, tourists flocked to Mount St. Helens by the thousands. They hoped to see the volcano erupt.

Scientists knew better. They were monitoring a growing bulge on the north side of the mountain. Pressure was building within the volcano. **Seismometers** recorded thousands of small **earthquakes**. Earthquakes can be a sign of an upcoming eruption. Scientists had park officials set up a 20-mile (32-km) safe zone around the mountain. Their planning saved many lives when the volcano exploded.

Dome

A scientist photographed the lava dome that formed on Mount St. Helens in 2004.

St. Helens Today

Scientists continue to study Mount St. Helens very closely. In October 2004, a dome of lava appeared inside the crater. The dome kept growing over the next three years. Today, the volcano is safe enough for hikers to climb its slopes.

Did You Know?

David Johnston was a **volcanologist**, or volcano expert. He was one of many who studied Mount St. Helens before its 1980 eruption. His efforts helped save many lives. He was the first to report the eruption on May 18. Sadly, he was killed in the blast.

#5
Mount Etna
Europe's Most Active Volcano

Mount Etna towers high above the island of Sicily in Italy. It is the tallest volcano in Europe. Over the past 3,500 years, it has erupted more than 250 times! The most violent of Etna's eruptions in 2007 shot lava 1,300 feet (396 m) high and covered nearby towns in ash. Most eruptions have been mild, but Etna has a long history of destruction.

FAST FACTS

Mount Etna

Location: Sicily, Italy

Type: Shield volcano

Height: 10,991 ft (3,350 m)

Last Eruption: 2008

Atlantic Ocean

Italy

ASIA

Etna

AFRICA

Red-hot lava poured out of Mount Etna during its 2001 eruption.

Going With the Flow

Etna's most destructive eruption happened in 1669. On March 11, lava began gushing from a 7-mile (11.3-km) **fissure**, or crack, in the mountain. The river of lava soon poured over the walls surrounding the city of Catania. The lava flooded the harbor. The eruption continued for nearly four months and destroyed 12 villages.

More Destruction

Etna's eruption in November 1928 destroyed Mascali, another of the many towns along its slopes. The fast-moving lava flows wiped out every building in town.

Etna's 1669 eruption buried more than 14 square miles (36 sq km) in lava.

Staying Active

Etna's earliest eruptions date back 300,000 years. Scientists think Etna began as an underwater volcano. It has grown and changed shape over time. Each eruption adds new layers of lava to the mountainside.

Volcanoes can be active, dormant, or extinct. Mount Etna is very active. An active volcano has erupted in the last 10,000 years and is expected to erupt again. A dormant volcano is "sleeping" but might erupt in the future. An extinct volcano won't erupt again.

Main crater

Vents

The International Space Station took this photo of Etna erupting in 2002.

Etna Up Close
Mount Etna is one of the most studied volcanoes on Earth. Volcanologists get very close to the action. They wear special fireproof suits when taking lava samples.

Locals watched Etna's slow-moving lava flow in 2001. The volcano's many eruptions are a fact of life for people in the area.

Fighting the Flow

Many people live on Etna's mountainsides. Tourists go there to ski. Farmers depend on the volcano's fertile ash for good crops.

The people of Sicily have tried many ways to stop Etna's lava flows. They have built trenches and dams to change the lava's path. Planes have dropped water to slow the lava flows. People have even set off dynamite to redirect the lava. Most of these attempts have had only limited success. Still, people in the area show no signs of moving away.

Did You Know?

Etna has inspired many myths. Ancient Romans believed Etna was the forge used by Vulcan, the god of fire. Vulcan was the blacksmith to the gods. Ancient Romans believed lava flares erupting from the mountain were sparks from Vulcan's forge. His name became the word for volcano.

#6
Mauna Loa
World's Largest Active Volcano

In Hawaiian, *Mauna Loa* means "long mountain."
The name is fitting. The volcano measures 75 miles
(121 km) from its sides to its peak. It covers nearly half
of the island of Hawaii, or "the Big Island." Mauna Loa
has erupted 15 times since 1900. Its lava flows have
swallowed roads and villages in their paths.

FAST FACTS

Mauna Loa

Location: Island of Hawaii

Type: Shield volcano

Height: 13,681 feet
(4,170 m) above sea level

Last Eruption: 1984

Pacific Ocean

Hawaii

NORTH AMERICA

Pacific Ocean

Hawaiian Islands

Mauna Loa

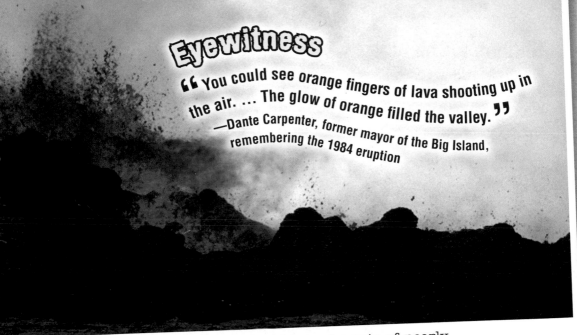

" You could see orange fingers of lava shooting up in the air. ... The glow of orange filled the valley. "
—Dante Carpenter, former mayor of the Big Island, remembering the 1984 eruption

In March 1984, Mauna Loa spewed lava at a rate of nearly 9 million gallons (34.1 million liters) a minute!

What a Blast!

On June 1, 1950, sleeping villagers on Hawaii's west coast got a rude awakening. Mauna Loa erupted with a roar heard 15 miles (24 km) away. Within three hours, lava had overrun the village. Luckily, everyone got out alive.

Mauna Loa's most recent eruption was in March 1984. Fountains of lava spurted from openings along its sides. In no time, rivers of lava burned their way toward Hilo, the island's largest city. Fortunately, the lava stopped 4 miles (6.4 km) short of the city.

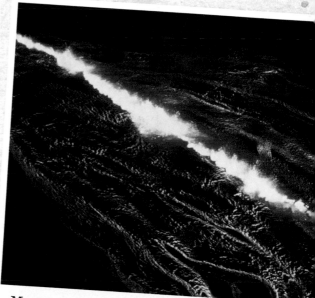

Mauna Loa's lava looked like a river of fire as it flowed toward Hilo.

Building a Shield

Mauna Loa is a shield volcano. This type of volcano forms when lava gently flows from a vent on the surface. The hardened lava forms a low, flat mound that looks like a shield.

Types of Lava

Mauna Loa has produced two types of lava. Aa (ah-ah) lava is chunky and thick and has a jagged surface. It moves very slowly. When this lava cools, it can be razor sharp.

Aa lava

Aa lava is made up of broken lava blocks called clinkers.

Pahoehoe (pah-HOY-hoy) lava often looks like wrinkled skin or coiled rope. It is thinner and moves faster than aa lava.

Pahoehoe lava

Pahoehoe lava moves forward in globs that break out from under cooled crust.

Hot Spot

Hawaii is a chain of islands formed by volcanoes. Hawaii is far from plate boundaries, where volcanoes usually form. The islands formed over a **hot spot**. There, magma rises from deep within Earth and hardens. With each eruption, the volcano gets bigger. Over time, it gets tall enough to break through the ocean's surface.

During the 1984 eruption, volcanologists used helicopters to get close to the lava flows.

Mauna Loa

Largest Volcano

This satellite photo shows the Big Island of Hawaii. Mauna Loa is the largest of five volcanoes that make up the island. The Big Island is the youngest in Hawaii. It appeared on the surface of the Pacific Ocean about 400,000 years ago.

Did You Know?

Mauna Loa stands 13,681 feet (4,170 m) above the surface. Measured from its base on the ocean floor, it stands more than 56,000 feet (17,170 m). This makes it much taller than Mount Everest, the tallest mountain on land.

Mount Everest

#7

Kilauea
World's Most Active Volcano

Kilauea is the youngest of five volcanoes that form the island of Hawaii. Each year, millions of tourists visit Kilauea. They hope to see its amazing lava flows up close. The volcano doesn't disappoint. Kilauea has been erupting since 1983. But the volcano isn't just a tourist spot. Kilauea is also the deadliest volcano in the United States. Its lava flows have wiped out entire towns.

FAST FACTS

Kilauea

Location: Island of Hawaii

Type: Shield volcano

Height: 4,190 feet (1,277 m) above sea level

Last Eruption: erupting since 1983

Pacific Ocean

Hawaii

NORTH AMERICA

Pacific Ocean

Hawaiian Islands

Kilauea

Rivers of Fire

On January 3, 1983, lava fountains burst from Kilauea. Since then, the eruption has expanded. The volcano's constant lava flows have destroyed nearly 200 buildings. About 9 miles (14 km) of road is buried under lava up to 80 feet (24 m) thick. Lava flows continue to threaten homes in the area.

Lava erupts from Kilauea. The volcano's name is the Hawaiian word for "spewing."

In 1990, lava flows from Kilauea destroyed the town of Kalapana.

A Good Study

Kilauea is one of the most studied volcanoes in the world. Because it is so active, scientists are always collecting new data. They also test monitoring equipment on the volcano. By learning more about volcanoes, they hope to save people from future eruptions.

A volcanologist studies glowing magma through a hole on the surface.

A Growing Island

Hawaii is expanding, thanks to Kilauea. Its lava flows have added about 500 acres (202 hectares) to the island. Lava and volcanic ash cool to form new, fertile land. Volcanic ash is rich in minerals that help plants grow.

Ferns grow in hardened lava near Kilauea.

Tourist Attraction

Kilauea is located in Hawaii Volcanoes National Park. Visitors flock to the park to see the volcano in action. They marvel at the slow-rolling lava. Visitors can get close enough to hear the hiss of steam as the molten river meets the ocean.

Lava from Kilauea falls into the Pacific Ocean. It flows about 7 miles (11 km) before it reaches the coast.

Did You Know?

Pele is the Hawaiian goddess of volcanoes. According to legend, she lives inside Kilauea. Many people believe that Pele curses anyone who removes volcanic rock from Hawaii. A park ranger at Hawaii Volcanoes National Park is rumored to have started this myth. He hoped to stop people from taking pieces of rock home with them.

#8
Yellowstone Caldera
Earth-Changing Eruptions

Yellowstone National Park is filled with natural wonders. Visitors hike past bubbling mud pools and hissing steam vents. They gasp when hot water shoots high into the air. These are reminders that the park sits on top of one of the world's largest volcanoes. It is sometimes called a supervolcano. The last Yellowstone eruption spewed ash over half of the United States.

FAST FACTS

Yellowstone Caldera

Location: Idaho, Montana, Wyoming

Type: Caldera

Height: 9,200 feet (2,805 m)

Last Eruption: 640,000 years ago

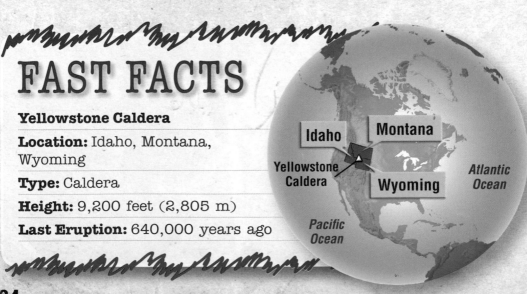

Idaho

Montana

Yellowstone Caldera

Wyoming

Atlantic Ocean

Pacific Ocean

Tourists

This huge hot spring is one of Yellowstone's many incredible features. It is heated by an underground supervolcano.

A Supervolcano Forms

Some of the largest volcanoes on Earth are calderas. They form when the top of a magma chamber collapses. This leaves a caldera, or a large bowl-shaped crater. About 640,000 years ago, a huge eruption formed the youngest of Yellowstone's three calderas. Together, they make up a crater that covers 1,300 square miles (3,367 sq km).

Yellowstone National Park is home to a lot of wildlife. These bison are grazing near a gushing steam vent.

Yellowstone's last eruption blasted ash as far away as Louisiana. Gases and ash clogged the air. Temperatures cooled around the world.

Measuring Eruptions

About 60 volcanoes erupt each year. However, only the biggest eruptions get much attention. How do scientists measure the power and size of an eruption? They use a scale called the Volcanic Explosivity Index (VEI). Volcanoes are rated on a scale of 1 to 10. A volcano with a VEI of 0 is non-explosive. The last eruption of Yellowstone was an 8.

Volcanic Explosivity Index

Here's how the last eruption of Yellowstone compares with others in this book.

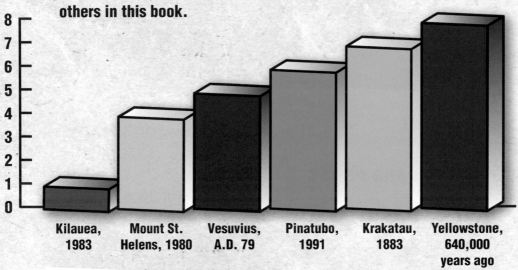

| Kilauea, 1983 | Mount St. Helens, 1980 | Vesuvius, A.D. 79 | Pinatubo, 1991 | Krakatau, 1883 | Yellowstone, 640,000 years ago |

Heat from Yellowstone Caldera creates natural rock terraces in Yellowstone National Park.

Bubble, Bubble, Toil and Trouble

A huge magma chamber bubbles below the surface of Yellowstone. The magma and hot rocks boil groundwater. This creates many amazing features. In some places, hot water bubbles to the surface in hot springs or pools. In other spots, **geysers** shoot steam and boiling water into the air.

Old Faithful
There are more than 300 geysers in Yellowstone National Park. The most famous is Old Faithful. The geyser shoots jets of steam and water about 130 feet (40 m) into the air about every 90 minutes.

Did You Know?

What would happen if Yellowstone were to erupt again? Most living things within hundreds of miles would be killed. One scientist says the whole United States would be covered with 5 inches (12.7 centimeters) of lava.

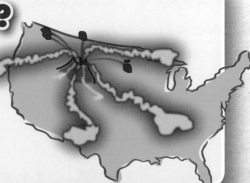

Mount Pinatubo
A Sleeping Mountain Awakens

In early 1991, nearly 1 million people lived around Mount Pinatubo. The volcano had barely rumbled for 450 years. No one recalled the mountain ever being a threat. Many even doubted it was a volcano. By June of that year, there was no question. Pinatubo roared back to life in a big way. Its eruption was the second biggest of the 20th century.

FAST FACTS

Mount Pinatubo

Location: Luzon Island, Philippines

Type: Composite volcano

Height: 5,248 feet (1,600 m)

Last Eruption: 1994

ASIA

Luzon Island

Pinatubo

Philippines

Pacific Ocean

Indian Ocean

AUSTRALIA

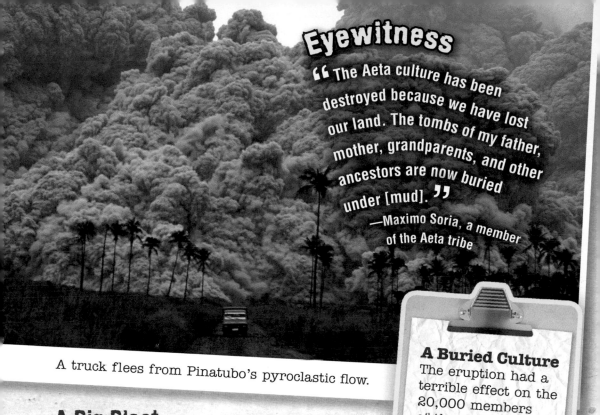

A truck flees from Pinatubo's pyroclastic flow.

A Buried Culture

The eruption had a terrible effect on the 20,000 members of the Aeta tribe. The mountain was their home. The eruption forever changed their traditional culture and way of life.

A Big Blast

After a week of small eruptions, Pinatubo exploded on June 15. A giant ash cloud shot 22 miles (35 km) into the air. The eruption produced a deadly pyroclastic flow. Hot ash rolled down the mountain like an avalanche.

Hours after the eruption, a **typhoon** hit. The rain mixed with ash in the air. It fell to the ground like heavy mud, collapsing rooftops. Heavy rains also turned volcanic ash into deadly mudslides. Moving like liquid concrete, the mud buried everything in its path.

Buildings on Luzon Island were buried under a mixture of ash and mud.

Whole Lot of Shaking Going On

In all, about 300 people died in the eruption. Thousands more would have died if they had not left the area. They owed their lives to scientists who saw the warning signs.

The first sign of trouble came on April 2, 1991. Steam exploded from the volcano's crater. Scientists measured the amount of **sulfur dioxide** gas produced by the volcano. High gas levels are a sign that an eruption is likely.

Volcanologists check a tiltmeter set on the side of Mount Pinatubo.

Tiltmeter

Scientists placed **tiltmeters** on the mountainsides. These instruments measure changes in the tilt, or angle, of the ground. Magma inside the volcano may cause the ground to bulge. Seismometers tracked earthquake activity. Thousands of small quakes were recorded in the months before the eruption.

A week after the eruption, ash still blocked sunlight. People covered their faces as they fled their villages.

Cooling Down

Pinatubo's eruption had a global impact. Gases from the eruption caused temperatures to drop by about 1° F (0.5° C) for the next two years. In the Northern Hemisphere, summers were cooler and winters were warmer.

More Mud

Pinatubo's 1991 eruption had a lasting effect. Each rainy season brought fresh mudflows created from Pinatubo's rock and ash. Some areas have been buried in mud up to 30 feet (9 m) thick. These later mudflows caused more damage than the original eruption did.

In September 1994, mudflows from Pinatubo were still a major problem.

Did You Know?

Pinatubo's eruption was the world's biggest since 1912. Yet it was smaller than many of the volcano's previous eruptions. The largest took place more than 35,000 years ago. The volcano was once as high as 7,550 feet (2,301 m). Today, it stands 5,248 feet (1,600 m). Its caldera is now a lake.

#10
Parícutin
Earth's Youngest Volcano

Most volcanoes are hundreds of thousands of years old. Parícutin is Earth's youngest. It first appeared in 1943, rising up from a cornfield in central Mexico. It gave scientists a rare chance to witness the birth of the volcano—and its death. In its short life, Parícutin taught scientists much about how volcanoes form.

FAST FACTS

Parícutin

Location: Parícutin, Mexico

Type: Cinder cone

Height: 1,391 feet (424 m)

Last Eruption: 1952

Pacific Ocean

NORTH AMERICA

Mexico

Atlantic Ocean

Parícutin

People watched as Parícutin erupted in 1947. Lava and ash had killed all the trees and plants in the area.

A Volcano Is Born

On February 20, 1943, a Mexican farmer noticed a crack had opened on a small hill on his land. As he watched, the hill began to rise. Smoke and ash escaped from the growing hole with a loud hiss. The smell of rotten eggs filled the air. A volcano was born.

Lost in Lava

As the volcano grew, so did the danger to nearby villages. Parícutin began spewing lava and raining ash that covered 100 square miles (259 sq km). Local people fled before their villages drowned in a sea of lava and ash. The eruption didn't end until 1952. At that point, the volcano was 1,200 feet (366 m) high.

Eyewitness

" I felt a thunder, the trees trembled, and it was then I saw how, in the hole, the ground swelled and raised itself 2 or 2.5 meters high. "
—Mexican farmer Dioniso Pulido, describing the appearance of the volcano Parícutin on his land

Hardened
lava

Parícutin stands behind the steeple of a damaged church. The church was built in the 1500s. The volcano's lava flows covered the rest of the church and every other building in nearby towns.

Growth Spurt

Parícutin grew quickly. Within a day of cracking through the surface, it stood 165 feet (50 m). The eruption added layers of volcanic ash to the growing mound. In just a week, the cinder cone was 460 feet (140 m) high. After one year of life, the volcano stood 1,100 feet (335 m) high.

Short Life

Its growth slowed over the next eight years. The volcano stopped growing on February 25, 1952. Parícutin is not expected to erupt again.

Mexico's Volcanoes

There are 22 volcanoes in Mexico. The tallest is Popocatepetl, an Aztec name that means "smoking mountain." At 17,887 feet (5,452 m) high, it is the second-highest volcano in North America.

Popocatepetl is a composite volcano that has been active for centuries. It is located just 34 miles (55 km) from Mexico City, the country's largest city. A big eruption could threaten the lives of millions of people. So far, its eruptions have been fairly mild.

Thousands of Mexican villagers moved away from Popocatepetl during its 2000 eruption.

Did You Know?

No one was killed directly by the eruption of Parícutin. But three people died from lightning strikes. Volcanic eruptions often trigger wild lightning displays. In 2007, scientists also discovered that the mouth of a volcano crackles almost constantly with low-energy lightning.

Honorable Mentions

Mont Pelée, Martinique

The 1902 eruption of Mont Pelée was the deadliest of the 20th century. The volcano produced an avalanche of hot volcanic rock and ash. The avalanche destroyed St. Pierre, Martinique's largest city. Only two people survived. More than 28,000 were killed.

Nevado del Ruiz, Colombia

Snow-covered Nevado del Ruiz erupted on November 13, 1985. Its pyroclastic flow melted the snow. That created a deadly mudslide that roared 60 miles (97 km) down the mountain. About 23,000 people lost their lives.

Olympus Mons, Mars

Earth isn't the only planet with volcanoes. The largest volcanoes in our solar system are on Mars. Olympus Mons is the biggest. It covers about 350 miles (563 km) in diameter and rises about 17 miles (27 km) high. Earth's largest volcanoes are no more than 6 miles (10 km) high and 75 miles (121 km) across.

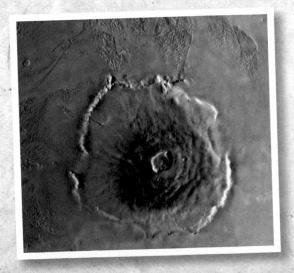

Glossary

archaeologists: scientists who dig up ancient objects and study them to learn about the past

artifacts: human-made objects from the past

caldera: a bowl-shaped crater in Earth's surface that forms when a volcano collapses

crust: the outermost layer of Earth

earthquakes: sudden movements in Earth's crust caused by a great release of pressure

fissure: a crack in Earth's surface

geysers: natural springs that shoot fountains of steam and boiling water into the air

hot spot: an extremely hot underground area that lies close to the surface

lava: molten rock from a volcano or a break in Earth's surface

magma: molten rock below Earth's surface

pyroclastic flow: an extremely hot mixture of ash, gas, and volcanic rock that travels at high speed down the sides of a volcano

seismometers: instruments that measure the vibrations of Earth at specific locations

sulfur dioxide: a type of gas produced by a volcano

tectonic plates: huge pieces of Earth's crust that move and slide near one another

tiltmeters: instruments that measure the angle of Earth's surface

tsunamis: giant ocean waves that are created when the seafloor moves because of erupting volcanoes or large earthquakes

typhoon: a powerful, whirling storm that brings strong winds and heavy rains

volcanologist: a scientist who studies volcanoes

For More Information

Books

Bauman, Amy. *Earth's Crust and Core* (Planet Earth). Pleasantville, N.Y.: Gareth Stevens, 2008.

Gazlay, Suzy. *Be a Volcanologist* (Scienceworks!). Pleasantville, N.Y.: Gareth Stevens, 2008.

Rubin, Ken. *Volcanoes & Earthquakes* (Insiders). New York: Simon & Schuster Children's Publishing, 2007.

Van Rose, Susanna. *Volcanoes and Earthquakes* (DK Eyewitness Books). New York: Dorling-Kindersley, 2004.

Web Sites

Volcanoes: The Earth at Work!
www.efieldtrips.org/cfm_bin/vv_altWindow.cfm?q_ID=HAVO

FEMA for Kids: Volcanoes
www.fema.gov/kids/volcano.htm

Publisher's note to educators and parents: Our editors have carefully reviewed these web sites to ensure that they are suitable for children. Many web sites change frequently, however, and we cannot guarantee that a site's future contents will continue to meet our high standards of quality and educational value. Be advised that children should be closely supervised whenever they access the Internet.

Index

About the Author

Jayne Keedle is a freelance writer and editor. Born in England, she lives in Connecticut with her husband, Jim; stepdaughter, Alma; a chocolate Lab named Snuffles; and Phoenix the cat.